WHERE FOOD COMES FROM

BEE TO HONEY

Sarah Ridley

WAYLAND

www.waylandbooks.co.uk

Thank you to Colchester beekeeper, Alan Hayden-Case, for his help with this book.

First published in Great Britain in 2018
by Wayland
Copyright © Hodder and Stoughton, 2018
All rights reserved
Editor: Sarah Peutrill
Designer: Matt Lilly
ISBN: 978 1 5263 0604 3

Printed and bound in China
Wayland, an imprint of
Hachette Children's Group
Part of Hodder and Stoughton
Carmelite House
50 Victoria Embankment
London EC4Y 0DZ
An Hachette UK Company
www.hachette.co.uk
www.hachettechildrens.co.uk

Picture credits:
arlindo71/Istockphoto: front cover t, 1t,9. temmuz can arsiray/Istockphoto: 2, 17, 19, 24l. BirdofPrey/Istockphoto: 18. Marc Bruxelle/Istockphoto: 20tr. Scott Camazine/Alamy: 14. Simon Colmer/Nature PL: 11. Dragisa/Istockphoto: 16. Gregory Dubus/Istockphoto: 20bl. Tom Gowanlock/Shutterstock: 3cr. Imo/Istockphoto: 23tr. Kaanates/Istockphoto: 23tc. T. Kimura/istockphgoto: 23br. Evan Lorne/Shutterstock:. 21tr Nattika/Shutterstock: 23cr. Stefa Nikolic/Istockphoto: 4, 5. Olgysha/Shutterstock: 22. Photogal/Shutterstock: 23bl. Photografiero/Istockphoto: 8. Photografiero/Shutterstock: 10. Proxyminder/Istockphoto: 6b, 12. Real444/Istockphoto: 23cl. sumikophoto/Shutterstock: 15. Sergey Sushitsky/Shutterstock: 13. Tienduong/Dreamstime: 7cl, 7tr, 24tr. Samo Trebizan/Shutterstock: 3bl. Tim UR/Shutterstock: 23tl. Valentyn Volkov/Shutterstock: 1b, 3tl, 21l. John Williams RUS/Shutterstock: 6t. Slawomir Zelasko/shutterstock: front cover b.

Every attempt has been made to clear copyright.
Should there be any inadvertent omission please apply
to the publisher for rectification.

Words in bold like **this** are in the glossary on page 24.

Honey is a sweet, sticky food.

honey

honeycomb

We eat it in yoghurt, on bread, and in cakes and biscuits.

But where does honey come from?

3

Honey is made by honeybees.

The bees live inside hives owned by beekeepers.
Some beekeepers own many hives, while others
have one or two hives in their garden.

A hive has several layers that lift off. When a beekeeper checks a hive, he or she wears special clothes to protect against bee stings.

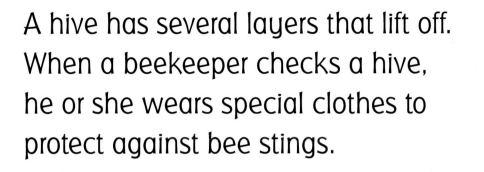

bees

As the air warms up in the morning, some of the honeybees start to leave their hive to look for food.

The bees fly from flower to flower searching for nectar and **pollen.**

This bee can smell the nectar inside the purple flower.

She sucks up the nectar into her **honey stomach.**

7

Another honeybee visits some **blossom**. As well as nectar, she collects pollen, cramming it into pollen baskets on her back legs.

WONDER WORD:
POLLEN

Pollen is made by the male part of a flower called the **stamen**. Bees feed pollen to their young.

On this close-up photo you can see
the different parts of a honeybee.

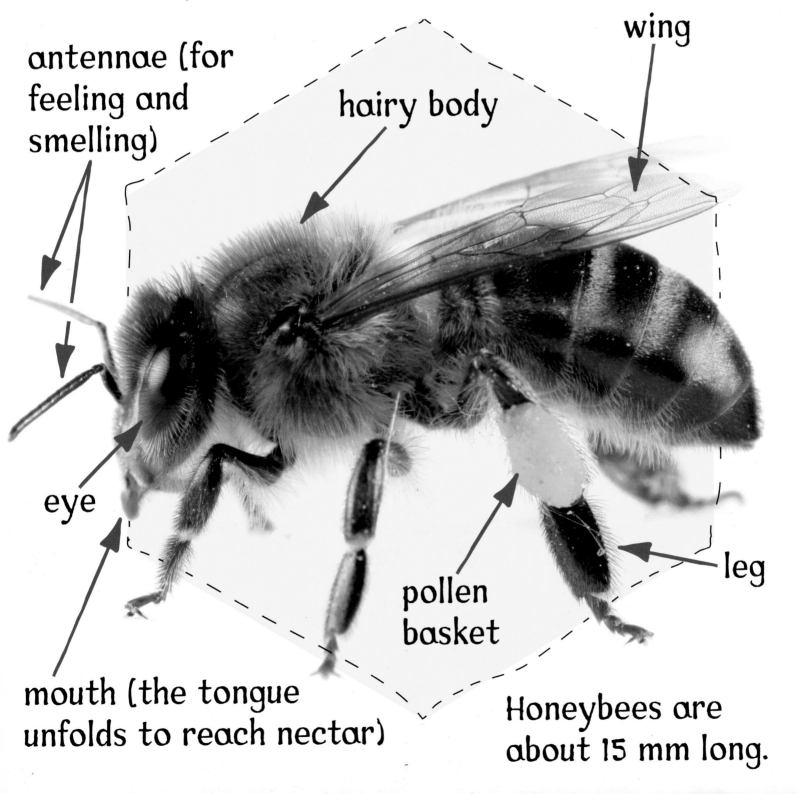

antennae (for
feeling and
smelling)

wing

hairy body

eye

mouth (the tongue
unfolds to reach nectar)

pollen
basket

leg

Honeybees are
about 15 mm long.   9

The bees collect more and more nectar until it is time to fly back to the hive to unload.

BEE FACT

A honeybee visits between 50 and 100 flowers on each trip.

Inside the hive, the bees pass the nectar from one bee to the other and slowly turn it into honey.

11

Honeybees store honey in the wax cells of a **honeycomb**. They fan the honey with their wings to make it lose some water and become thicker, and to make it stay fresh.

wax lid

honey in cell

When the honey is ready, they seal the cells with wax. Honey is their food over the winter months.

Honeybees build wax cells inside frames provided by the beekeeper. The frames hang next to each other inside the hive.

Before these bees set off to collect some more nectar, they notice that another bee has started to dance!

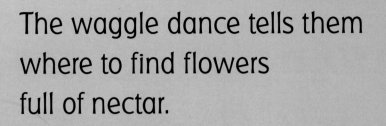

The waggle dance tells them where to find flowers full of nectar.

This bee sets off to collect the nectar. She makes about ten trips back to the hive before the end of the day.

BEE FACT

honey

In her lifetime of about 40 days, a honeybee will collect enough nectar to make about one twelfth (1/12) of a teaspoon of honey.

15

All the bees in one hive are called a
colony. The queen bee controls the colony
and lays eggs, which hatch into larvae.

queen bee

16

WONDER WORD:
LARVAE

Many insects,
amphibians and fish lay
eggs that hatch into
young called larvae.

Worker bees feed plant pollen to the larvae. They grow and grow, each in its wax cell. After a few weeks the larvae change into young bees.

larvae

BEE FACT

In the summer, a colony can grow to about 50,000 bees.

During the summer, honeybees usually make
so much honey that beekeepers can collect some.
To make the bees calm, a beekeeper puffs
some smoke from a smoker at the hive.

smoker

This frame of honeycomb is full of honey. The beekeeper will take it home to **extract** the honey.

19

First, the beekeeper uses a tool to scrape off the wax lids made by the bees.

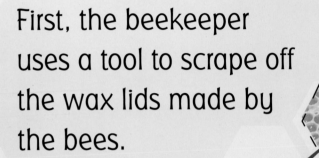

Then the beekeeper puts the honeycomb frames into a spinner. Spinning the honeycomb makes the honey run out.

The honey flows out of the spinner and through a sieve to catch any bits of wax.

Sometimes honey is heated to keep it runny. The beekeeper pours the honey into jars and the honey is ready to eat!

BEE FACT

In honey factories, honey is extracted from honeycomb in a similar way, using bigger machines.

21

As well as making honey, bees help plants to make seeds and fruit. While they are collecting nectar and pollen, pollen grains get stuck to their hairy bodies.

Some of the pollen brushes off on the female parts of the next flower the bee visits. This allows pollination to happen.

strawberries

almonds

kiwi fruit

apple

All sorts of plants are pollinated by bees and other types of insect. Many of these plants grow the fruit and vegetables that we like to eat, as well as the flowers in our gardens and countryside.

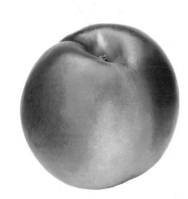
nectarine

Without bees, less would grow and it would be a big problem for people to fix.

sunflower

runner beans

WONDER WORD:
POLLINATION

Pollination takes place when the male part (pollen) of one flower reaches the female part of another, allowing it to make a seed or fruit.

23

Which shape are the wax cells where bees store honey?

Triangle, square or hexagon?

INDEX

beekeepers 4–5, 13, 18–21

colony 16–17

extracting the honey 19–21

hives 4–6, 10–11, 13, 15–16, 19

honeycomb 3, 12–13, 19–21

larvae 16–17

nectar 6–11, 14–15, 22

parts of a honeybee 9

pollen 6, 8, 11, 17, 22–23

pollen baskets 8–9

pollination 22–23

queen bees 16

smokers 18

spinners 20–21

waggle dance 14–15

wax cells 12–13, 17

GLOSSARY

blossom Another word for the flowers of trees or bushes.

extract To remove.

gland A part of an animal's body that produces a substance that the body needs to work properly.

honey stomach A special stomach where a honeybee stores nectar.

honeycomb Hexagons of wax cells made by bees to store honey and their young.

pollen A powder made by the male part of a flower.

stamen The male part of a flower.

BEE FACT

Honeybees collect nectar from about two million flowers to make one 454 g jar of honey.